The Christmas Tree Angel

Radio Drama

by Lisa Soland

All Original
Play Publishing

THE CHRISTMAS TREE ANGEL RADIO DRAMA
Written by Lisa Soland
Copyright © 2000 by Lisa Soland

Published in 2024 by All Original Play Publishing
P.O. Box 32381
Knoxville, TN 37930
AllOriginalPlays@gmail.com

First Edition: May 2024
Printed in the United States of America
Graphic Design by All Original Play Publishing
Back cover photo by Steven L. Sears

ISBN: 978-1-956218-37-4
Library of Congress Control Number: 2024908839

What they're saying about
THE CHRISTMAS TREE ANGEL RADIO DRAMA...

The original cast recording: Chris Durmick (Soldier), Andy Eichner (Mr. Brown), Melanie Ewbank (Mrs. Brown), Julie Maddalena Kliewer (Angel), Chip Chalmers (Pastor/Director), Lisa Soland (Narrator), Joe Russell (King/Camel) Brianne Siddall (Tommy), and unseen, Steven L. Sears (Clown/Lamb) who also took this photo.

The Christmas Tree Angel Radio Drama is dedicated to the compassionate Chip Chalmers, Melanie Ewbank, Brianne Siddall, Andy Eichner, Julie Maddalena Kliewer, Steven L. Sears, Joe Russell, and Chris Durmick.

These talented individuals were the pioneers who recorded the story late one night for children with special needs to enjoy during the Christmas season.

CAST of CHARACTERS

RADIO ANNOUNCER: An adult male, highly energetic.

FOLEY: An adult male or female with excellent timing.

NARRATOR: An adult male or female. Great reader. Expressive. Terrific storyteller.

PASTOR NELSON: An adult male, comforting.

MRS. BROWN: A 30 to 40-year-old woman, very loving.

TOMMY: A 7-year-old boy with much enthusiasm.

MR. BROWN: A 30 to 40-year-old man, fatherly.

ANGEL: A young girl.

CLOWN: A young girl or boy.

WISE KING: A young boy.

LAMB: A young girl or boy.

SOLDIER: A young boy to be paired with Angel.

CAMEL: A young girl or boy who can speak very slowly.

SINGERS: Three would be ideal, like the Andrew Sisters. Dressed in WWII-era dresses and hairdos.

SNOWFLAKES: At least three, but as many as you are able. Dressed in a white leotard, ballet slippers, and unique white snowflake attire with glitter.

PLACE

There are three playing areas on stage:

1. The NARRATOR'S living room with a wingback chair and fake fireplace.
2. The BROWN'S living room with a large Christmas tree and three mics on stands.
3. The FOLEY area with all the necessary sound makers assembled within reach.

TIME

The Radio Show takes place during WWII, but the story they share is set in 1899, at the turn of the century.

ACT ONE: Christmas Eve and Christmas Morning
ACT TWO: Christmas Afternoon

"The Christmas Tree Angel
Radio Drama"

by Lisa Soland

Starring...
HENRY POLIC II
as the "Narrator"
&
the Bethel School Children

☆☆☆☆☆☆☆

Directed by Lisa Soland

Musical Direction
Candace Rowland

One Show Only

December 16, 2004
7:00 PM
Free Admission

BETHEL LUTHERAN CHURCH & SCHOOLS
17500 Burbank Blvd. Encino, CA 91316
For more information phone (818) 788-2653 or visit the website at:
BethelLutheranChurchEncino.org

---

*Flyer from the original live production with the original live cast,
starring Henry Polic II, and directed by Lisa Soland.*

THE CHRISTMAS TREE ANGEL RADIO DRAMA received its world premiere on August 15, 2004, as the cast and crew gathered in the recording studio of the TV show *Scrubs* at 12629 Riverside Drive, Valley Village, California. Chip Chalmers directed, Joe Foglia was the Engineer, and Scott Brewster was the Assistant Engineer.

The cast was as follows:

PASTOR NELSON .... Chip Chalmers
MRS. BROWN .... Melanie Ewbank
TOMMY .... Brianne Siddall
MR. BROWN .... Andy Eichner
ANGEL .... Julie Maddalena Kliewer
CLOWN .... Steven L. Sears
WISE KING .... Joe Russell
LAMB .... Steven L. Sears
SOLDIER .... Chris Durmick
CAMEL .... Joe Russell
NARRATOR .... Lisa Soland

THE CHRISTMAS TREE ANGEL RADIO DRAMA received its world premiere live stage performance on December 16, 2004, at Bethel Lutheran Church in Encino, California. Lisa Soland directed the play, Vincent Archer stage managed, Lynn Campion choreographed the *Snowflakes*, and Nicole L. Schroud designed the costumes.

The cast was as follows:

NARRATOR .... Henry Polic II
PASTOR NELSON .... Criag Ayers
MRS. BROWN ....Joy Kilpatrick
TOMMY .... Daniel Rojas
MR. BROWN .... Brian Barnett
ANGEL .... Joele Sleezer
CLOWN .... Amber Beasley-Allen
WISE KING .... Ryan Dominguez
LAMB .... Jasmonae Cardin
SOLDIER .... Cody Barton
CAMEL .... Casey Engstrom
SNOWFLAKES .... Emme Lehmann Boddicker,
        Ashley Sunde, Rachel Rabska, Alayne Taylor, Chloe
        Szalai, and Bailey Stock
HEAD FOLEY .... Kevin Kruse
FOLEY .... Vili Lehmann Boddicker and Thomas Perez
PIANIST .... Edie Lehmann Boddicker

THE CHRISTMAS TREE ANGEL RADIO DRAMA was then produced as part of the Christmas Eve Service at the Ventura Center for Spiritual Living in Ventura, California, on December 24, 2012, and then again on December 24, 2023.

In the Ventura Center for Spiritual Living production, animals were invited to join the actors on the stage at the end of the performance.

THE CHRISTMAS TREE ANGEL RADIO DRAMA then had its Southeastern premiere at the Lyric Theatre Company in Loudon, Tennessee, on December 5, 2014. Robert Harrison produced the play, which was directed by Marie Fertitta. Donna Zukowski designed the costumes, and Stacy Littleton stage managed the production. The Incredible Christmas Place and Wampler's sponsored the production.

The cast was as follows:

RADIO ANNOUNCER ……..…….…………….. Tommy Parris
SINGERS ………………..……… Beth and Courtney Brakebill
CELEBRITY NARRATORS … Bill Landry and Sam Venable
FOLEY ……………………………………. Robert Harrison
PASTOR NELSON …………..…………….. Doug Thompson
MRS. BROWN …………..……………..….…. Crystal Lytle
TOMMY ……………………….…..…..…… Gabriel Miller
MR. BROWN ……………..…..……….. Jeremiah Wampler
ANGEL ……………………………………. Ieshia Presnell
CLOWN ……………………..…………… Sarah Williams
WISE KING …………….………………… Tavius Presnell
LAMB …………………………………… Shay McDonell
SOLDIER …………………..…..……..…… Simeon Thress
SNOWFLAKES ……..…… Emory McDonell, Alyssa Miller, and Felicity Gourley
BOY NARRATOR READS STORY TO …...… Lucas Gourley
CAMEL ………………………………..….…. Zoe Sibley

Southeastern Premiere Cast: Top Row: Beth and Courtney Brakebill, Crystal Lytle, Robert Harrison, Bill Landry, Tommy Parris, Doug Thompson, & Jeremiah Wampler. Bottom Row: Alyssa Miller, Felicity Gourley, Emory McDonell, Zoe Sibley, Ieshia Presnell, Simeon Thress, Lucas Gourley, Shay McDonell, Sarah Williams, Tavius Presnell, and Gabriel Miller. (Photo by: Julie Gourley)

THE CHRISTMAS TREE ANGEL RADIO DRAMA was again produced at the Lyric Theatre Company, premiering December 3, 2015. It was produced by Robert Harrison and co-directed by Robert Harrison and Sean Cowen. Charlene Bledsoe and Lori Loper designed and built the costumes. The technical team was Erica Ammons and Wheat Bailey, with Kaelyn Russell as stage manager.

The cast was as follows:

RADIO ANNOUNCER ………..…..…..…….. Sean Cowen
SINGERS (Thurs/Fri) ..….Rylee Kate Lorenz and Davis Boals
SINGERS (Sat) ….....…. Beth Brakebill and Courtney Brakebill
SINGERS (Sun) ….....…… Kaelyn Russell and Rachel Scheffer
NARRATOR ………………………………….. Doug Thompson
FOLEY …………………………………………… Kayce Bailey
MRS. BROWN (Thurs/Fri) …………………..…..….. Lisa Reves
MRS. BROWN (Sat/Sun) …………………….. Michele Miller
TOMMY …………………………………………. River Bailey
MR. BROWN …………………………..…………. Ed Fendley
ANGEL (Thurs/Fri) …………………………. Rachel Scheffer
ANGEL (Sat/Sun) ………………….……….. Rylee Kate Lorenz
CLOWN (Thurs/Fri) ………..……………… Yasmin Karimian
CLOWN (Sat/Sun) ………………………..……… Abby Hawkins
WISE KING ……………………………………… Gabe Miller
LAMB (Thurs/Fri) …………………………….……… Abigail Zell
LAMB (Sat/Sun) …………………………….. Arianna Edwards
SOLDIER (Thurs/Fri) …………………….…… Wheat Bailey
SOLDIER (Sat/Sun) ……………………..…………… Davis Boles

SNOWFLAKES ....…...… Crews Boals, Cricket Miller, Jackson Miller, Landon Parsons, Claire Zell, and Arianna Edwards
CAMEL (Thurs/Fri) ....… Kaelyn Parsons
CAMEL (Sat/Sun) ....….… Ella Breaux

THE CHRISTMAS TREE ANGEL RADIO DRAMA was produced for a third time at the Lyric Theatre Company, opening on December 1, 2016. Robert Harrison produced and directed, and Kaelyn Parsons stage managed. Charlene Bledsoe and Lori Loper designed the costumes, and Erica Ammons and Nathanael Parsons designed the lights and sound.

The cast was as follows:

RADIO ANNOUNCERS …....…… Jodi Moody and Jo Beliles
SINGERS ……………. Kaylen Lindsey, Carrie Arp Waltman, Alisa Inman, Nancy Owen, Rylee Kate Lorenz, Haley McNally, and Trinity Lee Anne Murphy
NARRATORS ....…......…Lisa Soland, Dr. Kim Miller, Marie Fertitta, and Alisa Inman
FOLEY ....…..… Alisa Inman and Tina Brunetti
PASTOR NELSON ....…......……….. Doug Thompson
MRS. BROWN ......… Jessica Danielle Rhoten and Lora Bolt
TOMMY ....… Austin Percival and Aiden Carman
MR. BROWN ....…..… Chris Thomas and Kenny Edmonds
ANGEL ....… Kaelyn Parsons and Trinity Lee Anne Murphy
CLOWN ....…..…… Marissa Finger and Rylee Kate Lorenz

WISE KING ..….…….…. Haun Zheng and Landon Carman
LAMB ..….……… Annabelle Garcia and Makenna Edmonds
SOLDIER ….…………. Preston Waggoner and Gabe Miller
SNOWFLAKES ….…..……… Gavin Cedillo, Jackson Miller,
    and Alana Finger
CAMEL ….…….…….. Carrie Thomas and Haley McNally

Notes from the Playwright

The Snowflakes are not necessary. The lines referring to them can simply be read by the narrator. But, if you have a dance troupe in town with little children, it enhances the production visually and will increase your audience.

You do not need the Radio Announcer character but using him helps to actualize the "play within a play" aspect. You can simply begin with the story's narration. You do not need the singers either, but if you have a business in town that has helped to finance your production, it takes little effort to rewrite a few of the "Jingle Bell" lyrics using their name.

It is recommended that you include public-domain Christmas song lyrics in your program and encourage your audience to join in the singing at the end of the show. After all, it's Christmas!

You do not need a live pianist to play the background Christmas music for the escaping snowflakes or to accompany the audience at the end, but again, it can be lovely if you have an enthusiastic musician available to play for your show.

The play runs about an hour, so depending on your needs and facility, you may implement an intermission or not. The shortened version of this play is available upon request. Email AllOriginalPlays@gmail.com.

(Note: nothing else in this copyrighted script can be rewritten, removed, or edited in any way as per your signed agreement.)

Introduction
and Acknowledgments

The Christmas Tree Angel was written at Christmas time, just before the turn of the century. While creating the story, I read it chapter by chapter to my family, who had gathered together to celebrate the birth of Jesus. I am grateful to my parents, Ann and Norman, and my brother Bryan and his family for receiving the new words with love and encouragement.

The story was then shared with my husband during our courtship in 2001, but it wasn't until Christmas of 2003 that the promise of a larger audience began to take form. Our friend Chip Chalmers suggested that we not exchange store-bought gifts, but instead, he played a beautiful song on his guitar, and I read *The Christmas Tree Angel.* Chip loved the story and recommended that we cast the characters and record it as a radio drama that would benefit children with special needs during the holiday season.

In August of 2004, the cast and crew gathered in the studio of the TV show *Scrubs* and recorded the story. Joe Foglia and Scott Brewster helped add sound effects. We received donations to copy the CDs and distributed them to the Braille Institute, Starlight Starbright Children's Foundation, Ronald McDonald House, and the Los Angeles Children's Hospital.

I want to thank Chip for his graciousness and all the actors who gave of themselves with no financial reward: Chris Durmick, Andy Eichner, Melanie Ewbank, Julie Maddalena Kliewer, Joe Russell, Brianne Siddall, and Steven L. Sears, who also photographed the event.

The live stage production of *The Christmas Tree Angel Radio Drama* premiered on December 16, 2004, to a sold-out audience at Bethel Church in Encino, California. I would like to personally acknowledge the late Henry Polic II, who brought the role of the narrator to life with his unique voice and talent. His contribution was invaluable, and I am forever grateful. I also want to thank actors Joy Kilpatrick, Brian Barnett, Kevin Kruse, my stage manager Vincent Archer, and all those involved in supporting the original production. Theatre is most assuredly collaborative; without them, the story could not have been told.

Today, the angel of our story finds her way to the first edition of the published actor's copy of the live radio drama. She will then make her way into other theaters and productions of your making, helping your communities celebrate the birth of Jesus Christ. May God richly bless you this holiday season and all the Christmases to come.

Lisa Soland (May 2024)

DESCRIPTION

The Christmas Tree Angel Radio Drama is a delightful play-within-a-play that's suitable for all ages. It can be produced with minimal rehearsal, a small cast, and a small budget. The story begins on Christmas Eve when the Brown family receives an angel ornament from their local pastor. Once the angel is placed on the tree, she meets new friends and learns that they will all be placed in boxes and stored in the attic until next year. The angel refuses to accept this fate, and with the help of her new friend, the soldier, she devises a plan to escape the darkness for good!

―――――――――――

The Christmas Tree Angel Radio Drama is a full-length play that runs under an hour without an intermission, so it can be performed with or without one.

A minimum cast includes:

3 ADULT MEN
3 BOYS
1 GIRL
3 BOYS OR GIRLS
2 ADULT MEN OR WOMEN
1 ADULT WOMAN

For greater participation, the cast may also include:

2 to 3 SINGERS
3 or more CHILDREN DANCING SNOWFLAKES
VERY YOUNG BOY & GIRL LISTENERS

THE CHRISTMAS TREE ANGEL
RADIO DRAMA

ACT ONE

SETTING: *A wingback chair sits downstage right, with a braided oval rug downstage of it. An antique radio sits on a small table beside the chair. Just upstage of the chair is a faux fireplace with stockings hanging in place. The Brown family playing area is upstage center, with three microphone stands that contain working mics. Behind them is a large, decorated Christmas tree. The foley table is located stage left. On the table should be all the sound-making equipment required for the story, along with a table mic to pick up the created sounds.*

RADIO ANNOUNCER: *(Enters.)* Welcome boys and girls, moms and dads, to the Lyric Theatre Sound Stage [Replace with the name of your theatre.] in beautiful downtown Loudon, Tennessee. [Insert the name of your town and state.] Before we begin, allow me to point out the exit signs in the event of an emergency and notify you that no photography is allowed during the performance. This evening [or afternoon], we will be recording live before your very eyes *The Christmas Tree Angel Radio Drama*, starring celebrity actor Bill

1

Landry [insert the name of your actor performing the role of Narrator]. This is our applause sign…

(Holds up applause sign.)

…and when I hold it up like this…

(HE does.)

…all of you need to applaud with great enthusiasm. Let's give it a try, shall we? Are you ready?

(HE holds up the sign, and the audience applauds.)

Impressive. Now, this over here is our "on the air" light. When this lights up, everyone in the audience must be very quiet. Should we try that, too? Are you ready backstage? Okay, light—on!!!

(The audience is very quiet.)

Excellent!

Raise your hand if this is your first time watching a radio drama being recorded live.

(Encourages folks to raise their hands.)

You will see the actors and hear them reading lines, but you will also see the sound effects being created. Does anyone know what is required to *see the story* in your mind?

(Encourages answers.)

Yes, that's right. This type of storytelling requires that you use your "*imagination*." So now, with your imagination on high alert…

(Glances at watch or clock on the wall.)

…please turn off any devices that could make noise during our recording.

(Takes a quick overview of the audience.)

Actors in place?

(ACTORS & FOLEY all improvise their acknowledgments.)

RADIO ANNOUNCER: Terrific. Thank you. Here we go now. Quiet in the sound stage.

(He looks at his watch or clock and counts down.)

Ten, nine, eight, seven, six, five, four, three, two...

(The "On the Air" light comes on, and the RADIO ANNOUNCER now uses his/her full radio voice.)

Welcome ladies and gentlemen, to the Christmas Special Radio Hour. This evening [or afternoon], we will be recording live from the Lyric Theatre Sound Stage in beautiful downtown Loudon, Tennessee, *The Christmas Tree Angel Radio Drama.* Now, let's all give a very warm welcome to actor Biiiiiiiill Landry! [Use your actor's name.]

(RADIO ANNOUNCER holds up applause sign and NARRATOR enters from offstage and takes a bow. HE sits in the NARRATOR'S chair downstage right, followed by small CHILDREN in their pajamas. The CHILDREN sit on the floor in front of the seated NARRATOR.)

RADIO ANNOUNCER: Today's performance is sponsored by The Christmas Gallery! [Replace this with those who finance your production.]

(HE holds up the applause sign, and the audience applauds.)

(Background music begins, and SINGERS enter. When they arrive at the mics, they begin the jingle sung to the tune of Jingle Bells.)

SINGER ONE: THE CHRISTMAS STORE
SINGER TWO: RIGHT NEXT DOOR.
SINGER ONE: GIFTS BEYOND COMPARE.
SINGER TWO: ALL YOUR CHRISTMAS SHOPPING
NEEDS…
SINGER ONE: …JUST RIGHT OVER THERE.
SINGER TWO: WHERE?

SINGER ONE: THE CHRISTMAS STORE,
SINGER TWO: WELL, WHAT FOR?
SINGER ONE: GIFTS ONE OF A KIND.
SINGER TWO: CREATED BY AN ARTIST'S HAND.
BOTH: THE CHRISTMAS GALLERY.

RADIO ANNOUNCER: *(Holds up applause sign.)*
Thank you, Lyric Studio Singers. Yes, The Christmas
Gallery. Everyone on your shopping list will be happy
Christmas morning to unwrap an original gift from
The Christmas Gallery, and you'll be supporting your
local artists. So, a big heartfelt thanks to The
Christmas Gallery for being our sponsor for today.
(Holds up applause sign again.)
Now, ladies and gentlemen in our sound stage and
those listening from your living rooms at home, sit
back, relax, and enjoy tonight's [this afternoon's]
performance of The Christmas Tree Angel Radio
Drama, starring Bill Landry.
(RADIO ANNOUNCER holds up applause sign,
then, when applause starts to die down, points to
FOLEY to begin.)

FOLEY: WINTRY WIND, SOFT AT FIRST, THEN GROWING

NARRATOR: Once upon a holiday time, in a snow-covered Christmassy town, an ornament was delivered as a gift of good tidings to the Brown family who lived on the hill. The local pastor, upon giving the little angel, gave of his heart as well, and a little more light was in the room than there was before.

PASTOR NELSON: The merriest of Christmases to you, Mrs. Brown. May this angel bring you and your family peace and protection.

NARRATOR: He patted her hand and then parted, for the night was blustery, and he had many more stops to make.

FOLEY: CREAKING DOOR, THEN WIND GETS LOUDER, THEN CLOSING DOOR

NARRATOR: *(Continuing.)* Mrs. Brown shivered as she closed the door and gathered the hand-knit shawl tightly to her chest.

MRS. BROWN: Burrr! I don't remember a colder Christmas Eve. I hope we have enough wood for the fire.

NARRATOR: Still holding the ornament in her hand, she called to her son.

MRS. BROWN: *(Calling out.)* Tommy! We have a new ornament! One more ornament for the tree!

FOLEY: BOY WITH PADDED FEET RUNNING ON HARD WOOD

NARRATOR: The boy ran into the room, dressed in his red
and green flannel pajamas. Moist chocolate still
lingered above his lip. Mrs. Brown smiled at the sight.
Hot cocoa was the perfect remedy for a child's
anxious Christmas wishes.

TOMMY: Oh boy, Mom. Let me! Here, I'll do it! Let me put it
on the tree.

FOLEY: BOY JUMPING UP AND DOWN

MRS. BROWN: All right, Tommy. But stop jumping and
catch your breath. You'll need to be gentle. This angel
is such a special addition to our Christmas tree.

NARRATOR: She placed the delicate angel into his trembling,
little hands, and up and onto the tree it went...

FOLEY: TINY BELLS & BRANCHES

NARRATOR: *(Continuing.)* ...but only as high as Tommy
could reach, which was about four feet, two inches on
a good night of stretching. *(Beat.)* Mrs. Brown
carefully lit each candle on the tree, and together,
mother and son stepped back to look at the results of
their labor. But how could something this fun be
thought of as labor? This was true Christmas spirit.
They looked forward to it all year through. Why, just
this afternoon, the blacksmith from town dropped the
tree off at their doorstep, and now, before them, stood
a fully decorated Christmas tree, lit up like a forest of
synchronized fireflies.

TOMMY: Gee, playing with the ornaments sure was fun.

MRS. BROWN: Doesn't it look lovely?

TOMMY: Can we take them all off and do it again?

MRS. BROWN: *(Laughing.)* I don't think so, young man. It's time for you to go to bed.

TOMMY: Ohhh, Mom. Can't I stay up just a little while longer?

NARRATOR: Tommy had cuddled himself around the bottom of the tree and was gazing upward through its scented boughs. He had already secretly examined most of the presents, searching for a special something. What he really wanted couldn't possibly come in such small, ordinary packages. His perfect present would need to be bolted and screwed together. The wheels would need to be oiled, and the red paint shined. A bicycle! He longed for one so dearly. His dreams had him riding on blue-lined clouds every night since his father announced that Christmas was on its way again.

MRS. BROWN: You need to go to bed now, honey.

TOMMY: How 'bout I sleep here, under the tree?

FOLEY: BRANCHES MOVING.

MRS. BROWN: We've already talked about this, Tommy. It's Christmas Eve, and we must give Santa enough time to leave his blessings.

TOMMY: I was a good boy this year, wasn't I, Mom?

MRS. BROWN: Yes, you were—most of the time. Now off you go, young man.

NARRATOR: Mrs. Brown patted Tommy on his plaid-covered bottom, and he scampered down the hall.

FOLEY: BOY RUNNING OUT OF ROOM WITH PADDED FEET.

NARRATOR: Mrs. Brown smiled once more at the pastor's fine gift, carefully blew out each candle on the tree... *(MRS. BROWN blows out the imaginary candles.)* ...and then retired for the evening. In the still of the night a key turned in the front door.

FOLEY: A KEY TURNING IN A DOOR, DOOR OPENING, THEN HEAVY FOOTSTEPS

NARRATOR: Mr. Brown stepped through the doorway, bundled in layers of warm clothing. He peeled them off as he stood on the welcome mat, knocking the snow from his heavy, black boots.

FOLEY: KNOCKING BOOTS ON HARD WOOD, THEN DOOR CLOSING.

NARRATOR: *(Continuing.)* As he crossed through the room, a flicker of light from the tree caught his eye.

MR. BROWN: Mrs. Brown! How could she have left a candle burning on the tree? A sure chance for a fire!

NARRATOR: He drew in a breath, ready to blow out the burning light...
(MR. BROWN takes in a deep breath, ready to blow.)

NARRATOR: *(Continuing.)* ...but there was none. No candle. No flame was left burning. Only a Christmas angel ornament he had not seen before. She seemed to be smiling back at him and beaming white light.

FOLEY: ANGEL BELLS

NARRATOR: Mr. Brown could not understand why he had to smile while looking at her. All he knew was that his heart was glad. *(Beat.)* He yawned…

FOLEY: OVEREXAGERATED YAWN

NARRATOR: *(Gives FOLEY a look.)*
…and then checked in on Tommy. For a moment, he watched his son sleeping and was amazed at how fast he was growing into a fine young man. He then knelt beside Tommy's bed and kissed him.

FOLEY: A KISS

MR. BROWN: *(Softly with affection.)* Good night, my precious boy.
NARRATOR: Mr. Brown stoked the embers still burning in the fireplace of the bedroom he shared with Mrs. Brown.

FOLEY: POKING A PIECE OF WOOD WITH STEEL

NARRATOR: He then tucked himself beneath the warm quilt, cuddled up close to his wife, and fell fast asleep. Outside, all that could be seen moving on this sleepy night was a thin wisp of smoke rising from each of the three chimneys in the Brown's little home on the hill.

FOLEY: OBNOXIOUS SNORING

(MR. BROWN reacts to the over-exaggerated snoring sounds FOLEY is making.)

NARRATOR: *(Looks at FOLEY and then makes a cutting signal to quit with the snoring sound.)*
The room with the tree was *quiet…*

FOLEY: STOPS SNORING SOUND AND MAKES A SOFT WIND SOUND

NARRATOR: *(Smiling and nodding.)*
…as the angel recalled the long carriage ride and being carried into the Browns' home wrapped in a woolen blanket. She remembered the warmth in the heart of the man who brought her here. And she remembered a small boy placing her on the tall tree. She thought of this most of all because she felt his joy and his hope for things to come. *(Beat.)* Her eyes focused as she looked about the tree. Was she alone? Oh, she couldn't bear being alone after such a long journey. She turned her stiff neck and caught sight of a clown holding an orange balloon.

FOLEY: ANGEL BELLS

ANGEL: Hello there, jolly clown! And how might you be on this fine evening?
CLOWN: Oh, I'm jolly enough tonight, but tomorrow's eve will bring about another painted face on me—one of sorrow and sadness.
ANGEL: Why is that?

CLOWN: If you don't know, I'm not one to burst your balloon.

ANGEL: *(Confused.)* Burst my balloon?

NARRATOR: His remark seemed odd. She couldn't imagine life on this tree to be anything but joyful. She looked to the left and saw what seemed to be a wise man dressed in purple velvet.

FOLEY: ANGEL BELLS

ANGEL: *(Calling out to him.)* And how might you be this evening, Wise King?

WISE KING: This night is the best of all nights, so I am nothing but delighted. But it means very soon, darkness. Darkness to come.

ANGEL: Darkness?

WISE KING: Yes, a very long darkness with cold and nothingness for days.

NARRATOR: The little angel began to tremble.

FOLEY: TINY BELLS

NARRATOR: No matter which way she turned, she couldn't escape the warning words of trouble. She longed to feel once more the joy of the boy and the gentle touch of his mother. With these pleasant thoughts in her head, she was able to think more clearly.

ANGEL: I will climb! I will climb up this tree!

FOLEY: TINY BELLS AND BRANCHES CONTINUING THROUGHOUT HER CLIMB

NARRATOR: And she began to lift herself, reaching as far as she could, one wing at a time. It was difficult, for sure, but she was determined. She stretched her wing and then pulled some more.

FOLEY: TINY BELLS AND BRANCHES MOVING

NARRATOR: The voices frightened her as she climbed. And if the truth were known, it made the climbing rather difficult.

CLOWN: It won't make a difference, Miss Angel.

WISE KING: No matter how high you climb. It will still come to you.

NARRATOR: And if that wasn't enough, a cantankerous lamb, who hung on the tree not far from the others, put in her two bleats as well.

LAMB: You caaaan't escape the daaaarkness. All of us must faaaace it and soon.

NARRATOR: Their words fell hard upon her ears and caused her painted eyes to water, but her mind was made up. She had chosen to climb.

FOLEY: TINY BELLS AND BRANCHES MOVING

ANGEL: There must be something better on the top of this tree. At least from there I will be able to see things much clearer.

NARRATOR: Of course, wings aren't meant for climbing.

FOLEY: A PIECE OF CLOTH, TEARING

ANGEL: *(Climbing.)* Oh, dear.

NARRATOR: They tear, and they rip, and so they did on this delicate angel all the way up the Christmas tree.

FOLEY: TEARING

NARRATOR: But, though torn and weary, the little angel was happy because she was on her way. The angel was now on a journey of her own choosing.

ANGEL: *(Climbing.)* Almost there.

FOLEY: TINY BELLS AND BRANCHES

NARRATOR: The air grew cold in the room as the last bit of wood turned gray. The angel reached and strained for the last time.

FOLEY: SOUND OF CLOTH TEARING, THEN TINY BELLS

NARRATOR: Somehow, perhaps with the help of holiday spirit, the angel had climbed all the way up to the top of the tree. And she was right. Things were better here. She felt more comfortable sitting upon fewer boughs. Her white satin dress lay as it should, in a complete circle without bunching up.

FOLEY: TINY BELLS

ANGEL: This is where I was meant to be—on the top of the Christmas tree! What a very long journey I've had!

NARRATOR: Much to her dismay, little was left of her wings. Though the wire holding them fast to their form was still in place, the finely woven lace had suffered significant damage. Pieces hung hopelessly. Although the angel had never considered flight, the idea now seemed impossible. *(Beat.)* But she wasn't going to think of such things. She was too tired to face any more peril. It was time to rest. So, the little angel wrapped a branch around her midriff...

FOLEY: BRANCHES MOVING, TINY BELL

NARRATOR: ...and quickly fell asleep.
(Bright and cheery.)
Christmas morning comes the slowest of all mornings. The darkness of night refuses to change as if the entire world were closed inside a cardboard box. But come it did, as all mornings do. The Brown boy was up and bouncing like the sun into the room with the tree.

FOLEY: BOY BOUNCING UP AND DOWN WITH BARE FEET

NARRATOR: He screamed with delight when he spotted the red bike parked between the fireplace and the front door. A large green bow covered the silver handlebars.
TOMMY: Oh my gosh! I got it. I got my bike. Yippeee!
NARRATOR: As quickly as he appeared, Tommy was gone again, sliding his way across the hardwood floor on his way to wake up his mom and dad.

TOMMY: I got it. Santa left me a bike. Can I ride it? Can I ride it now, before breakfast, Mom?

NARRATOR: There was a moment of silence in the Browns' home. Two sleepy adults with tousled hair appeared in robes. Tommy dragged them toward his newfound treasure.

TOMMY: Look, Mom. Look, Pop. I must have been a very good boy. Look what Santa left me!

MRS. BROWN: I'll put on the coffee.

MR.BROWN: *(Clears his throat, stalling for time.)* Now, Tommy, Santa gave you this bike in hopes that you would be careful with it.

TOMMY: I will, Pop.

MR. BROWN: A bike like this is a little tougher to ride than that old tricycle of yours.

TOMMY: I know, Pop. I'll be careful.

MR. BROWN: Your mom or I need to be with you when you ride. Especially when you're first starting out.

TOMMY: Sure, Pop. I know.

NARRATOR: Tommy was growing bored with the drill. Just then, Mrs. Brown reappeared in the doorway.

MRS. BROWN: *(To Mr. Brown.)* I'm worried about him, honey. We live on a hill, and that will make it hard for him to learn.

TOMMY: I'll take it to the park, Mom. I'll walk my bike down the hill to the park and ride it there.

MRS. BROWN: We'll talk about this some more later. For now, how about we all sit down to a lovely breakfast?

MR. BROWN: What is that you're cooking in there, Mrs. Brown? Pancakes?

MRS. BROWN: Nooo.

TOMMY: French Toast?

MRS. BROWN: Nooo.

RADIO ANNOUNCER: It's…!

> *(RADIO ANNOUNCER holds up a sign that reads, "Wampler's Farm Sausage," and encourages the live audience to say it.)*

AUDIENCE/TOMMY/MR. BROWN: WAMPLER'S FARM SAUSAGE!!!

TOMMY: Yippppeeee!

RADIO ANNOUNCE: That's right, ladies and gentlemen. Mrs. Brown is cooking America's favorite sausage since 1937—Wampler's Farm Sausage.

> *(NARRATOR rises and stretches. RADIO ANNOUNCER brings him a glass of water, and he drinks as the SINGERS enter and stand at the mics upstage center. The following jingle can be found online.)*

SINGERS: WAMPLER'S, WAMPLER'S, IT'S GOOD SAUSAGE. MADE ON THE FARM IN TENNESSEE. DON'T SAY SAUSAGE, JUST SAY WAMPLER'S FOR THE BEST IN QUALITY.

ONE SINGER: *(Inviting the audience to sing, too.)* Everyone join in!

SINGERS: WAMPLER'S, WAMPLER'S, IT'S GOOD SAUSAGE. MADE ON THE FARM IN TENNESSEE. DON'T SAY SAUSAGE, JUST SAY WAMPLER'S FOR THE BEST IN QUALITY.

RADIO ANNOUNCER: *(Holds up applause sign.)*
That's right, Ladies and Gentlemen, Wampler's Farm
Sausage is a terrific way to start your Christmas
morning. Served proudly in homes throughout the
United States, all in a manner consistent with
Christian values and ethics. A family tradition since
1937; let it be yours. All of us at the Lyric Theatre
Sound Stage would like to thank Wampler's Farm
Sausage Company for sponsoring this segment of The
Christmas Tree Angel Radio Drama, and now…
*(RADIO ANNOUNCER looks to NARRATOR to see
if he's ready. NARRATOR nods and sits back down.)*
RADIO ANNOUNCER: …back to our story.
*(RADIO ANNOUNCER holds up applause sign,
then, when applause starts to die down, points to
the NARRATOR to go.)*
NARRATOR: The branches on most trees tend to thin out
toward the top. This is the very reason fewer
ornaments are hung there. From this spot, her spot, the
little angel had the pleasure of witnessing her first
Christmas morning. How blessed she was to
experience the pure joy of a child's heart. Happiness
filled her completely. Today was a brand new day. But
as soon as she found herself happy, the thought came
that she was alone. She turned her face to the left and
then to the right and noticed there was no one near.
She had climbed herself right into loneliness.

FOLEY: TINY BELLS

SOLDIER: *(Calling up to Angel.)*

Hello there!

NARRATOR: The angel heard a strong and kind voice.

SOLDIER: Good morning, and Merry Christmas!

NARRATOR: It must have been coming from below her
feet somewhere.

SOLDIER: Can you hear me?

NARRATOR: The angel thought of looking down, but the idea
frightened her. In fact, it made her tremble, though the
voice seemed pleasant.

SOLDIER: I said, up there. Can you hear me?

ANGEL: Why, yes. Yes, I can.

SOLDIER: I'm just below you. Over here, to the right.

ANGEL: *(Frightened.)* Oh, my!

SOLDIER: It's all right. You're anchored rather well on that
sturdy branch. Take a chance and look at me.

NARRATOR: The angel certainly thought the chance was
worth taking, for she could surely use a friend.

FOLEY: TINY BELLS

NARRATOR: She stretched her neck as far as she could, and
sure enough, at the base of her gown, a little over to
the right, hung a soldier. Quite handsome in his
appearance, and he was looking up at her, smiling.

SOLDIER: Well, good morning, and Merry Christmas to you.

NARRATOR: The colors he wore were not freshly painted
reds and blues as you might think. They were worn
and faded. But, like his voice, the soldier's face was
strong and kind.

ANGEL: *(Timidly.)* Merry Christmas to *you*.

NARRATOR: As she gazed at him, her cheeks grew quite warm.

SOLDIER: You're a genuine sight for sore eyes.

ANGEL: Who, me?

SOLDIER: *(Playfully.)* Is there any other angel up there on the top of this tree?

ANGEL: Why, no. There isn't. I suppose I'm it.

SOLDIER: *(Impressed.)* In all my life, I've never seen an ornament change their position as much as you. In fact, besides me, no ornament has ever moved from the position in which they were originally placed.

ANGEL: *(Surprised.)* Really?

SOLDIER: Certainly not. And it's a good thing. What would the family think if they came back into the room and none of the ornaments were where they put them?

ANGEL: I suppose you're right.

SOLDIER: I most certainly am. Everyone stays in their place because they're afraid to do anything other than what is expected of them. They never even suspect they can move themselves about. But I hear a lot of wishing going on.

ANGEL: What kind of wishing?

SOLDIER: Oh, your basic ornament wishes like, "I wish Mrs. Brown would come along and move us somewhere else." Or, "Gee, I wish Tommy was a tad taller. He hears us when we talk and he could put us wherever we want to go."

ANGEL: The boy can hear us?

SOLDIER: He can now, but that will come to an end in another year or two.

ANGEL: *(With sadness.)* I see.

SOLDIER: That was quite a climb last night.

ANGEL: Yes, and I have a little less the lace for it, I'm afraid

SOLDIER: Well, no worries. Mrs. Brown will mend you
before she puts you away for the year.

ANGEL: Away for the year?!

SOLDIER: Oh, yes. Mr. Brown is deathly afraid of a fire with
the candles burning on the tree. So, tonight's the night.
The old grandfather clock in the hall will strike six,
and the Brown family will begin to take down the
Christmas tree. All of us ornaments will be placed
back into our boxes and stored in the attic until next
year.

FOLEY: RUNNING WITH BARE FEET

NARRATOR: At that moment, Tommy reappeared and started
to examine the rest of the packages under the tree.

FOLEY: FIRMER STEPS WITH SLIPPERS

NARRATOR: His father trailed behind with more wood to add
to the fire.

**FOLEY: LOGS BEING PLACED ON FIRE,
CRACKLING**

NARRATOR: Soon, warmth filled the room again. Mrs.
Brown joined them, and together, they unwrapped the
presents and shouted and laughed. All the while,
thoughts spun inside the little angel's head.

ANGEL: Could this be true? Is it possible there is no use for me except for these two days a year? Is this the fate that awaits me?

NARRATOR: It didn't seem possible. An ornament filled with such love to give and no place to give it but to the inside of a box. She had so much to ask the soldier, who looked like he was enjoying the morning festivities. Had he actually lived through this dreary darkness? How could he bear it? How could he simply hang there on the tree, smiling, knowing what was to come? Buried alive. She was going to be buried alive.

FOLEY: TINY BELLS, STARTING QUIETLY THEN LOUDER

NARRATOR: The little angel had worked herself into such an anxious state that she almost shook herself right off the top of the tree when she heard another voice.

MRS. BROWN: Honey, did you move the angel to the top of the tree?

MR. BROWN: No, I did not. Where did she come from, anyway? I noticed her last night.

MRS. BROWN: Pastor Nelson paid us a visit yesterday. He brought the angel to us. Isn't she lovely?

MR. BROWN: *(Smiling with suspicion.)*

She looks especially good at the top of the tree. Very fitting for an angel, wouldn't you say? She can keep an eye on things from up there.

NARRATOR: It must have been Mr. Brown who moved the little angel to the top of the tree. Mrs. Brown leaned over to him on the sofa and softly kissed him.

FOLEY: MAKES THE SOUND OF KISS AND THEN GOES ON AND ON

(Both MR. and MRS. BROWN look at FOLEY.)

MRS. BROWN: You are a beautiful man, Mr. Brown. And I am so blessed.

MR. BROWN: So many toys could keep a young boy busy for a good, long time, Mrs. Brown.

MRS. BROWN: I think you're probably right, Mr. Brown.

NARRATOR: After such a busy morning, Mr. and Mrs. Brown retired to their room. And all that could be heard was the sound of wheels pushing against the hardwood floor.

FOLEY: WHEELS PUSHING AGAINST WOOD

TOMMY: This truck is great. Look at this. You push it hard into the ground three times and then see? It magically goes all on its own!

FOLEY: WHEELS PUSHING AND THEN DRIVING AWAY, AND THEN RUNNING INTO SOMETHING

NARRATOR: And so it did. In fact, the truck rode itself right into the side of Tommy's new bike.

TOMMY: Wow, this is great. Look at this bike. It has a basket for newspapers and a bell that rings and everything.

FOLEY: ONE RING OF A BIKE BELL

TOMMY: Did you see this bell?

FOLEY: TWO RINGS OF A BIKE BELL

NARRATOR: The angel wondered to whom the boy was
       speaking.

ANGEL: *(Whispered to SOLDIER.)* Who is he talking to?

TOMMY: I'm talking to you!

FOLEY: TWO RINGS OF A BIKE BELL

ANGEL: To me?

TOMMY: Yes, you. Did you see my new bike this morning?
       Did you notice how it shines?

NARRATOR: This was an amazing world. The angel never
       had the company of a child. She had been missing a
       precious experience and never knew it.

ANGEL: Yes, of course, I noticed.

TOMMY: Don't you like my bike, Angel?

ANGEL: It's a beautiful bike. You've certainly been blessed.

TOMMY: I am the most blessed boy on the hill.

ANGEL: But not so blessed to live on a hill.

TOMMY: *(Sadly.)* Oh, you heard my mom and dad?

ANGEL: They seem to be very concerned about you. They
       must love you very much.

TOMMY: I guess so.
       (TOMMY shrugs.)

FOLEY: ONE BIKE BELL

TOMMY: Look at these handlebars. I can't wait to ride it
       down the road. I'll be the best newspaper boy in town!

NARRATOR: He jumped onto the white leather seat and, using his foot to balance, half-pedaled his way around the room.

FOLEY: BIKE BEING RIDDEN, 3 TIMES IN A CIRCLE

NARRATOR: Tommy made three full turns and then dismounted. He tried to lower the kickstand, but it was hard to budge for such a small boy. Instead, he leaned the bike against the stone of the fireplace.

TOMMY: Angel, how did you get to the top of our Christmas tree? Did my pop move you there?

ANGEL: I climbed up all through the night.

TOMMY: You must be tired.

ANGEL: I am.

TOMMY: Are you having a nice Christmas? What did you get?

ANGEL: Oh, my. What did I get?
(She smiles.)
Why, I got you, Tommy.

TOMMY: *(Surprised.)* Me?

ANGEL: Yes, you.

TOMMY: *(Tickled.)* Gee! What do you know about that?! I gave you a Christmas present, and I didn't even know it! Fly down here, Angel. I want to give you a ride on my new bike.

ANGEL: *(Disbelief.)* Pardon?

TOMMY: *(Louder.)* I said fly down here. My parents are sleeping, and I'd like to give you a ride on my new bike!

NARRATOR: The angel's head spun. Was this possible?
Could she really leap off this tree?

TOMMY: I'd take you down myself, but I'm only this high.

NARRATOR: He held up his hand as tall as the hair on his
head to prove to the angel how impossible that task
would be.

TOMMY: Quick, hop off. I'll catch you. Here, look. I'll use
my new baseball glove.

FOLEY: HIT HAND INTO MITT TWICE

TOMMY: I was first baseman last summer. My pop gave me
this for my very own. It's big, so I can catch better.
Neat, huh?

NARRATOR: The angel thought perhaps she was dreaming.
Maybe she imagined this better future to avoid the one
described to her by the other ornaments. She blinked
her eyes again and again to force herself awake.

TOMMY: *(Impatiently.)* Are you coming or not?

ANGEL: *(Whispering to SOLDIER.)*
What should I do?

SOLDIER: *(Whispering back.)* What do you want to do?

ANGEL: My wings. They're torn. They won't work.
(Her voice cracks with emotion.)
I'll do nothing but fall.

SOLDIER: Well, you could stay and hope that we are put into
the same box together. The ornaments hung close to
one another on the tree usually end up in the same
box.

FOLEY: HAUNTING ECHO "THE SAME BOX, THE

SAME BOX, THE SAME BOX!" FADE OUT

NARRATOR: The words echoed in her ears. The same box, the same darkness, the same cold. What kind of a life is that? Even next to a friend, it's still darkness.

ANGEL: Why don't you come with me?

SOLDIER: No.

ANGEL: Why not? Come with me.

SOLDIER: That sounds doubly risky, don't you think?

ANGEL: So you don't think I can make it?

SOLDIER: *(Reassuringly.)* Angel, I believe you can do anything you put your mind to.

ANGEL: But what about my wings?

SOLDIER: They may surprise you.

NARRATOR: The angel closed her eyes, took a deep breath…

FOLEY: TAKES A BREATH

NARRATOR: …then turned back to Tommy, ready to jump, but he was gone.

FOLEY: TINY BELLS

NARRATOR: She'd taken too long to decide and lost her chance. If she had a heart beneath the pearl necklace and the satin dress and the carefully carved wood, it was breaking. It was breaking within her.

SOLDIER: Don't worry, pretty angel. He'll be back.

NARRATOR: The soldier was now standing right beside her. He had climbed up the rest of the way to comfort her, and now they stood side by side at the top of the tree.

SOLDIER: He'll be back. You'll see.

FOLEY: SOFT WIND

NARRATOR: The sun had now become part of the afternoon
　　　　　sky, and the room with the tree took on a different
　　　　　shade of light. With the angel's hand in his, the soldier
　　　　　spoke to her of his many adventures as they passed the
　　　　　slow hours of Christmas. Their exchanges differed
　　　　　from others that day. They gave each other gifts of
　　　　　storytelling, careful listening, and the comfort of a
　　　　　held hand. *(Beat.)* In the simplicity of this setting,
　　　　　Tommy bound in anew, wearing his Sunday best and
　　　　　looking for something fun to do.

FOLEY: CHILD RUNNING WITH DRESS SHOES

MRS. BROWN: Tommy, your galoshes are in the window
　　　　　seat.

**FOLEY: POTS AND PANS CLANGING AS IF
　　　　　COOKING**

NARRATOR: Mrs. Brown was roasting something wonderful
　　　　　in the kitchen. The smells of the delicious food filled
　　　　　the small home on the hill.
TOMMY: I don't want to go.
NARRATOR: Mr. Brown entered just in time to catch
　　　　　Tommy's words that were meant only for the walls
　　　　　and maybe the listening ornaments.
MR. BROWN: The choice is not for you to make, Son.

TOMMY: *(With head hung.)* I know, Pop.

MR. BROWN: Apologize and put on your overcoat.

TOMMY: I'm sorry.

NARRATOR: Tommy reluctantly pulled on the plain rubber boots but let the top of the window seat slam shut.

FOLEY: WINDOW SEAT SLAMMING SHUT

MR. BROWN: Tommy.

TOMMY: Oops. And I'm sorry for that too.

MR. BROWN: I'll help your mother with the turkey.

TOMMY: *(Calling out to his father as he goes.)*
Pop, can I take my bike to Grandma's?

MR. BROWN: *(Calling from the other room.)*
No, Son.

TOMMY: How 'bout something smaller?

MR. BROWN: Pocket size. Bring something that can fit into your pocket.

NARRATOR: Tommy wondered what Santa gave him that could possibly fit into the pocket of his woolly coat. There was the yellow dump truck that drove itself, the mitt, and the bike. But no, the bike had already been discussed.

NARRATOR: Tommy reached into his pocket and imagined the possibilities. It was rather deep and wide compared to his small, mittened hand.

TOMMY: Why, you could fit an apple pie in there if you weren't afraid of losing the filling. Angel? What are you planning for this afternoon? *(Beat.)* Angel? Are you awake?

NARRATOR: Just then, Mr. and Mrs. Brown came into the
room carrying the turkey and a pecan pie wrapped up
and ready for travel.

FOLEY: TWO SETS OF FOOTSTEPS ENTERING

MRS. BROWN: Thank you for dressing so quickly, Tommy.
MR. BROWN: What gift did you decide to bring, Son?
TOMMY: *(Still deciding.)* Uhhhmmm…this!

FOLEY: BRACHES

NARRATOR: Tommy pulled one of the largest red and white
candy canes off the Christmas tree.
TOMMY: Is this okay, Mom?
MRS. BROWN: Yes, Tommy. But wait until after you've
finished your Christmas dinner.
NARRATOR: The Browns bundled themselves up and opened
the front door, inviting in such a wind…

FOLEY: BLOWING WIND

NARRATOR: …that the snowflake ornaments could no longer
hold on to the tree.

SINGERS: *(THEY enter, stand by FOLEY, and sing.)*
**DECK THE HALLS WITH BOUGHS OF
HOLLY. FA LA LA LA LA, LA LA LA LA.**
*(THEY grow softer as NARRATOR comes in with
the next line.)*

'TIS THE SEASON TO BE JOLLY, FA LA LA LA LA, LA LA LA LA. DON WE NOW OUR GAY APPAREL, FA LA LA, LA LA LA, LA LA LA. TROLL THE ANCIENT CHRISTMAS CAROL, FA LA LA LA LA, LA LA LA LA.
(After the song, SINGERS exit.)

NARRATOR: The ornamental snowflakes danced about the room, and just before the Browns closed the door behind them, they blew out the front door and danced their way across the lawn, playing happily atop the real snowflakes of winter.

FOLEY: WIND, THE SOUND OF DOOR CLOSING, THEN BRANCHES MOVING

NARRATOR: Inside, the angel and the soldier had arranged several solid branches to lie on and had fallen fast asleep, still gently holding each other's hands as they napped. Sharing stories of their interesting lives had somehow brought them closer. Amongst all the newness of a busy world, they had found comfort in each other. No sounds from below could have disturbed them. *(Quietly.)* The tree was silent, and so was the home on the hill on this snow-white Christmassy afternoon.

(LIGHTS fade out.)

End of Act One

ACT TWO

NARRATOR: Sometimes, things you want to do are quickly followed by things you don't want to do. And so the cycle continues. For this is how living things grow— by work of both the sun and the snow. The Brown family returned home for the evening with Tommy's candy cane half eaten and Mr. Brown's belt loosened another notch.

FOLEY: DOOR OPENING, WIND, DOOR CLOSING

NARRATOR: The cool air from the opened door brushed across the angel's face, waking her from her nap.

MR. BROWN: How about you play some Christmas music on that new Victrola of yours, Mrs. Brown? And we'll all change into some comfortable clothes to take down the tree.

FOLEY: TWO OF THEM, LEAVING THE ROOM

NARRATOR: Father and son left the room, itching to get out of their wool suits. Mrs. Brown took a rare moment for herself and fondly gazed upon the tree for the last time.

MRS. BROWN: *(Whispering.)* If it were left to me, I'd leave you up all season long. It seems a shame to limit Christmas spirit to these two days a year.

NARRATOR: Mrs. Brown's words echoed in the angel's ears as if she had dreamed them.

MRS. BROWN: *(Echo-like.)* "It seems a shame to limit Christmas spirit to these two days a year."

FOLEY: TINY BELLS AND BRANCHES

ANGEL: Soldier. Soldier, wake up. The family's home, and I'm afraid.

NARRATOR: The soldier held the angel's hand a bit tighter.

SOLDIER: Somehow, I know that everything's going to be fine.

ANGEL: What time is it?

SOLDIER: There's no way of knowing until the sounds come from the hall.

ANGEL: The grandfather clock?

SOLDIER: Yes. That's right.

NARRATOR: This strong and kind soldier continued to comfort her, but the thought of what was to come did not. The angel trembled with no answers for the trial she was about to face.

FOLEY: TINY BELLS

ANGEL: Maybe we could climb down.

SOLDIER: There's no time for that now. It took you all night to climb up halfway. Remember?

ANGEL: Yes, but going down must be easier.

SOLDIER: You wouldn't make it.

ANGEL: Don't you mean *we*? *We* wouldn't make it?
(Silence.)
If there was a way to fix my wings, maybe we could fly. What do you think, my soldier?

LAMB: He thinks you taaaaalk too much.

NARRATOR: Then, something stirred from the other side of the tree.

FOLEY: BRANCHES

NARRATOR: A camel with one hump and four long legs appeared

CAMEL: *(Speaking very slowly.)* Well, hi there, you two. I've been listening to your dilemma.

LAMB: Who haaaasn't?

CAMEL: It took me all afternoon, but I finally got here. I think I might be the solution to your problem.

SOLDIER: If it took you all afternoon to climb around the side of this tree, how might you be the solution?

CAMEL: Haven't you ever heard of camel hair coats?

ANGEL: Why, yes. Everyone's heard of camel hair coats. But I don't need a coat.

SOLDIER: *(Impatiently.)* What she could use is a pair of wings. Do you happen to have a spare set in your saddlebags there?

CAMEL: Camel coats are made with camel hair. My hair. Why don't you use my hair to mend your wings?

SOLDIER: Now that might work!

NARRATOR: The moment their plan was set into motion, the grandfather clock in the hall began to chime.

FOLEY: INTRODUCTION TO CHIMING, THEN THE FIRST CHIME

SOLDIER: It could be only five o'clock.

CAMEL: Or it could be only four.

SOLDIER: You were awake, Camel. Did the clock already
     chime four or five?

FOLEY: 2ND CHIME

CAMEL: I don't know. I can only count to two.

NARRATOR: So, it was past two o'clock and before six, that
     much they knew. If it had been after six, the Browns
     would have taken down the tree, and the ornaments
     would already be in darkness.

FOLEY: 3RD CHIME

NARRATOR: The grandfather clock struck three as the
     ornaments held their positions on the tree. The silence
     between the chimes seemed endless. Then, the fourth
     sound rang out from the hall.

FOLEY: 4TH CHIME

NARRATOR: The angel wondered why she had never noticed
     these deafening noises before.

TOMMY: *(Spoken as if in the kitchen.)* Let's make some
     popcorn, Mom.

MRS. BROWN: *(As if in the kitchen.)*
     Oh, Tommy. We've just had dinner. Aren't you full
     from dinner?

TOMMY: No. See? I've got lots of room.
     *(TOMMY pulls the top of his pants out away from
     his body to prove his point.)*

It's Christmas Day, Mom. There's a lot of room for
wishes to still come true.

MRS. BROWN: I think you're right, Tommy. Let's make us
some popcorn.

TOMMY: Yippee. Thanks, Mom.

FOLEY: 5TH CHIME. THEN, POTS AND PANS

NARRATOR: The human voices filled the moments between
the fourth and fifth chimes. But the longest pause of
all was the one after the fifth. It was so long, in fact,
that the angel, the soldier, and the camel thought the
sixth sound would not come at all. But it did. Oh, but
it did.

FOLEY: 6TH CHIME

LAMB: I could haaaave told you it was six o'clock, but you
haaaad to draaaag it out, didn't you?

SOLDIER: Listen, the Browns decorate the tree the same way
every year—from the top to the bottom. But they un-
decorate it exactly the opposite of that—from the
bottom to the top. That should buy us some time. Let's
get to work and see how far we can get.

CAMEL: I'm game. *(Beat.)* But don't shoot me.
(A slow laugh.)

NARRATOR: With a nod from the angel, they began. The
soldier pulled out one hair at a time from the camel's
coat.

CAMEL: *(Lightly.)* Ouch!

NARRATOR: And then used it to tie together the shredded
lace of the angel's wings. Each time he pulled out a
strand, the camel let out an…

CAMEL: Ouch.

NARRATOR: So the soldier pulled, and the camel…

CAMEL: Ouched!

NARRATOR: And on they went.

CAMEL: That's smarts.

NARRATOR: And the Brown family appeared, one by one,
into the room with the tree. It seemed to be three
against three. A race against time.

CAMEL: Ouch!!!

NARRATOR: As Mrs. Brown cleared the presents from
beneath the tree, she spotted her holiday record, a gift
from Mr. Brown. Her husband cranked up the
Victrola.

FOLEY: WINDING UP THE VICTROLA

(SINGERS enter.)

NARRATOR: Mrs. Brown placed the needle on the spinning
groove, and the song rang out into the air.

**SINGERS: HARK, THE HERALD ANGELS SING,
'GLORY TO THE NEWBORN KING.'**
*(SINGERS continue to sing the rest of the song but
become quiet when the Narrator starts the next line.
SINGERS fade out when noted in stage directions.)*

NARRATOR: Although this song spoke of cheer, declaring
"peace on Earth and mercy mild," the angel felt no

peace in her heart. All she felt was the dread of the inescapable box, attic, and days upon days of darkness and nothingness and fear.

ANGEL: Faster. Faster!

NARRATOR: They had repaired one wing and were moving on to the next when the dreaded boxes were dragged into the room, scraping loudly against the hardwood floor.

FOLEY: WOOD BOXES BEING DRAGGED

NARRATOR: At the sight of them, the angel shook, which made tying knots on her wings even more difficult.

SOLDIER: *(Pleading.)* Please stop shaking.

CAMEL: *(Slowly, trying to calm the angel.)*
I've been with the Brown family for nearly 12 years now.

NARRATOR: The soldier understood what the camel was doing and joined in.

SOLDIER: Oh, really?

CAMEL: *(Slowly.)* Oh, yes. True story. I was tied to the top of a wedding present.

SOLDIER: Were the Browns married on Christmas Day?

CAMEL: Christmas Eve. I saw the entire ceremony from up here on the tree. It was quite moving, actually.

ANGEL: *(Crying out.)* Are you tying?

CAMEL: We're moving right along. No fret. No fret. Right along. *(Beat.)* Ouch.

NARRATOR: The camel tried hard to be cheerful, but Mrs. Brown and Tommy were already halfway up the tree.

37

LAMB: You knooooow, even if you turkeys maaaake it off
this tree, you're still going to eeeend up in the boooox.

FOLEY: BRANCHES

NARRATOR: Right then, the lamb was plucked from her [his]
temporary home amongst the branches.
TOMMY: Don't you ever have anything good to say, Lamb?
LAMB: Very nice weather we're haaaaving, don't you think?
NARRATOR: …and into the box she [he] went.

FOLEY: SLIGHT BANG

NARRATOR: The wise man was next to go.
WISE KING: The happiest of New Year's to you, Tommy, my
boy.
TOMMY: Why, thank you, King. And a very happy New Year
to you, too.
MRS. BROWN: Who are you talking to, Tommy?
TOMMY: The ornaments.
MRS. BROWN: The ornaments?
TOMMY: Yup.
NARRATOR: The three workers at the top of the tree stopped
to listen. Mrs. Brown took the record off the Victrola.
(SINGERS stop singing.)
TOMMY: They tell me how they're feeling and where they
want to go on the tree.
MRS. BROWN: And how long has this been going on?
TOMMY: Uhhhmmm. As long as I can remember.
NARRATOR: Mrs. Brown wondered how she should handle
this. She and Mr. Brown encouraged Tommy to have

his own thoughts, and creativity was always welcome in their little home on the hill, but she wasn't sure about talking to ornaments.

MRS. BROWN: *(To herself.)* This might be something to share with Mr. Brown. Two minds stand a better chance of choosing the right way to go.
(Calling out.)
Honey?

FOLEY: SPOON IN CUP, RATTLING

MR. BROWN: *(Calling from the kitchen.)*
I'm in here, making cocoa.

MRS. BROWN: *(To TOMMY.)* Tommy, why don't you play with your toys for a bit? I'll go help your father in the kitchen.

TOMMY: Okay, Mom. I can't reach any more ornaments by myself anyway.

NARRATOR: Tommy dropped to his knees and ran the yellow truck across the hardwood floor.

FOLEY: WHEELS RUNNING THREE TIMES INTO HARD FLOOR

NARRATOR: The camel, the soldier, and the angel went back to work, moving faster than ever. Tommy had borrowed them some time.

CAMEL: Ouch.

SOLDIER: Sorry.

CAMEL: Ouch.

SOLDIER: Sorry.

CAMEL: Ouch.

SOLDIER: Sorry!

TOMMY: *(Calling up to them.)* What are you three doing up there?

NARRATOR: The ornaments froze fast in place.

TOMMY: What's wrong, Angel? Why aren't you talking with me anymore?

ANGEL: Tommy. I'm having my wings fixed.

CAMEL: *(Quietly.)* Ouch.

TOMMY: What's wrong with them?

ANGEL: They ripped apart while I was climbing to the top of the tree.

TOMMY: I'm sorry, Angel. Does it hurt much?

CAMEL: Ouch.

ANGEL: Not for me, but I'm afraid the camel might be a little worse for wear.

CAMEL: Oh, I don't mind. Happy to give. Happy to give. *(Beat.)* Ouch.

ANGEL: Quite honestly, I'm glad to be whole again, Tommy.

TOMMY: My mom's in the kitchen. She's talking with my dad about me talking to you.

ANGEL: What do you think about that?

TOMMY: I think maybe I'm in trouble.

ANGEL: *(Worried.)* Oh, I wouldn't want that.

TOMMY: Me neither. That's about the only thing I'm afraid of.

ANGEL: I don't blame you for that.

TOMMY: What are you afraid of, Angel?

FOLEY: SOFT WIND

ANGEL: Boxes. I'm afraid of dark places and not being able to love.

TOMMY: I don't like dark places either. My parents let me keep the door open when I go to bed at night.

ANGEL: That must be wonderful.

TOMMY: Why don't you fly down here, Angel, and I'll keep you from the darkness, too.

NARRATOR: Oh, those words. Those beautiful words. Could she receive the gift of a second chance? She hoped and longed for the comfort of Tommy's care and a life beyond the box.

SOLDIER: *(Whispering to ANGEL.)*
Ask him how. Go ahead; ask him.

ANGEL: Tommy, how will you keep me from the box?

TOMMY: I don't know. I guess I'll tell my mom and dad that you're afraid.

SOLDIER: *(Whispering to ANGEL.)*
That won't work. They'll think he's making it up, and they'll discourage it.

CAMEL: *(Whispering.)* You'll end up in the box then, for sure.

TOMMY: *(Calling up to ANGEL.)* I have an idea. Why don't you fly down here and I'll put you on the handlebars of my bike.

FOLEY: ONE BIKE BELL RING

ANGEL: But what would be my purpose? I'm afraid I'll need a purpose, something other than simply sitting on the top of Christmas trees.

TOMMY: *(Thinking out loud.)* Well... I think purposes have something to do with what a person does best. What is it you do best, Angel?

NARRATOR: That was a very difficult question. She remembered the pastor who brought her here and how he offered her in hopes that she would bring peace and protection to the family.

ANGEL: Tommy! I have it! I will protect you on your bike through all your journeys.

TOMMY: That's good. Mom and Pop will like that. Come on now. Before they come back.

NARRATOR: The little Christmas angel quivered with happiness. She could both escape the box and do what she did best: protect and serve. Her heart, the one she most certainly had, leapt for joy inside her. *(Beat.)* But as quickly as she felt such great happiness, she thought of her friends standing beside her on the tree. Would her new journey include them, or would they suffer the fate she had feared?

ANGEL: What will you do, Camel? Will you join me?

CAMEL: Oh, no. Not me. I look forward to the long winter's nap. Besides, I have to grow my coat back.

NARRATOR: She [he] smiled a funny, crooked smile, then kissed the angel's rosy cheek.

CAMEL: This is my home and has been for a very long time. I'm comfortable here.

ANGEL: And my soldier? What will you do? Have you made up your mind?

SOLDIER: You know, I've never really found my home. And I never really thought of looking anywhere else until I met you, my angel.

NARRATOR: This made her smile, though it was not the
answer she'd hoped to hear from his painted mouth.
SOLDIER: So yes! I will come with you!

FOLEY: TINY BELLS

NARRATOR: The angel threw her wings around the soldier's
wooden neck.
SOLDIER: I suppose I should keep looking for my home until
I find it.
ANGEL: Oh. Thank you. Thank you so much!
NARRATOR: And knowing that a very little boy was waiting
for them, they paused no longer. The soldier took the
angel's hand tightly into his, and together they leapt
off the very top of the Brown's Christmas tree.

FOLEY: FALLING SOUND, USING A SLIDE WHISTLE

NARRATOR: Now, this was one incredible spectacle, let me
tell you—two Christmas ornaments with faces fully
beaming, soaring mid-air for they were free.

FOLEY: CONTINUING THE SLIDE WHISTLE...

NARRATOR: Actually, free-falling was more like it. No one
expected this. Of course, the angel didn't know if her
wings worked or not because they had never been put
to the test. But even if they did work, they were
probably meant to carry the angel alone, not the
soldier, too.

FOLEY: THE FALLING SOUND CONTINUES...

NARRATOR: *(Continuing.)* Much to their dismay, gravity
      was pulling them faster and faster toward the
      hardwood floor.

FOLEY: FALLING SOUND...

NARRATOR: *(Continuing.)* This is the very reason why
      baseball teams spring up all over small towns like this
      —so little boys can catch falling ornaments from off
      the top of Christmas trees. Tommy simply moved his
      arm out from behind him and on his left hand was his
      beloved glove. He caught them both softly and safely
      in his padded mitt.

**FOLEY: SOUND OF TWO ORNAMENTS LANDING
      IN A LEATHER GLOVE**

NARRATOR: And as he promised, Tommy tied the angel to
      the handlebars of his bike, right next to the bell.

FOLEY: TWO BICYCLE BELL SOUNDS

NARRATOR: And because he knew of the soldier's fondness
      for her, he placed him in the wire basket right next to
      where he imagined the newspapers would go. The
      three went for such a ride, around in circles through
      the room with the tree.

FOLEY: BIKE RIDING IN THREE CIRCLES, THEN TWO BICYCLE BELL SOUNDS

CAMEL: *(Laughing.)* You look like a silly circus act riding in those circles.
(ANGEL, SOLDIER, CAMEL, and TOMMY all laugh.)
NARRATOR: What an accomplishment this was for them.

FOLEY: TWO BICYCLE BELL SOUNDS

NARRATOR: It was quite lovely till Mr. and Mrs. Brown stepped back into the room.
MR. BROWN: We need to talk with you, Son.
TOMMY: Okay, Pop.
NARRATOR: Tommy brought his bike to a halt as his heart pounded in his chest.
MR. BROWN: Your mother tells me that you've been talking with these ornaments.
TOMMY: Yes, Father.
NARRATOR: Suddenly, Mrs. Brown, seeing the angel perched on the front of the bike, interrupted them.
MRS. BROWN: Tommy, how did the angel get down from the top of the tree?
NARRATOR: Tommy wondered if he should tell the truth. The angel wondered if she'd be boxed. And the soldier stood by, simply amazed by it all.
MRS. BROWN: That angel was at the top of the tree when I left this room.
TOMMY: Yes. I know, Mother.
MRS. BROWN: Well, how did she get down from there?

TOMMY: *(Simply.)* I told her to jump, and she did.

NARRATOR: There was silence in the room with the tree in the Brown home on the hill.

MRS. BROWN: *(In disbelief.)* You told her to jump?!

TOMMY: Yes.

MRS. BROWN: *(To MR. BROWN, quietly.)*

There is no way Tommy could have gotten that angel down from the top of that tree.

TOMMY: I didn't, Mom. She jumped. And I caught her with my glove. See?

FOLEY: HITS FIST INSIDE OF GLOVE TWICE

MR. BROWN: *(HE clears his throat.)*

Son, even parents sometimes must have faith in things we cannot see or hear. Do you understand what I'm saying, Tommy?

TOMMY: Yes, Father. You can't hear the ornaments, so you're trying to have faith.

MR. BROWN: *(Surprised by his son's wisdom.)*

Yes, that's right. Now you can see my problem. If what you're telling us is true, why then is it that the ornaments on the tree talk to you but not to us?

TOMMY: Because Father, you stopped listening long ago.

NARRATOR: At that moment, Mr. Brown remembered his own boyhood Christmas tree and how he, too, would sleep cuddled up beneath it so he would have a friend to talk to on Christmas Eve. He had forgotten all about his friends on the tree and also the importance of good conversation, sharing, and, most importantly, listening carefully to those you love. *(Beat.)* Mr. Brown looked

46

at the angel on Tommy's handlebars. She seemed to be smiling back at him…

FOLEY: TINY BELLS

NARRATOR: …beaming white light. And though he still could not put into words why he had to smile while looking at the little angel, he was glad. And that was enough.

MR. BROWN: Tommy?

TOMMY: Yes, Pop?

MR. BROWN: That angel sure is a special angel. Isn't she, Mrs. Brown?

MRS. BROWN: She sure is.

MR. BROWN: And furthermore, I think we should keep her around all year through.

TOMMY: Oh, Pop!

NARRATOR: Tommy threw his arms around his father's neck.

TOMMY: She is special, and she's going to protect me on my bike. She said so.

MRS. BROWN: Well, now, that's a worry off my mind.

MR. BROWN: And what about this ornament here, Son? What about this soldier standing at attention in the basket of your bike?

TOMMY: Well, the two of them are good friends, so they have to stay together.

NARRATOR: Tommy reminded his parents of the most important things in life—love, friendship, and staying together.

*(SINGERS enter and sing "Oh, Come All Ye
Faithful" lightly in the background.)*

NARRATOR: *(Continued.)* And so they did—the angel and
the soldier and Tommy. They stayed together all year
through—every year. And Tommy learned how to ride
that two-wheeled bicycle safely like it had been born
beneath him, which pleased his pop. They rode to the
park, to church on Sundays, and even down the hill on
which the Brown home stood. Tommy no longer
feared getting into trouble. The angel no longer feared
being put in a box. And the soldier found his home
amongst his true friends. *(Beat.)* It isn't every day an
angel is given as a gift of good tidings, but when the
gift is from the heart, anything is possible.
(SINGERS fade out on the song.)

**FOLEY: WIND BLOWING, then fade out during next
line**

NARRATOR: And so it was in the Brown home on the hill.
Like that first Christmas long ago, miracles reside in
the smallest of places and sometimes in the littlest of
angels.
*(We now see that the SMALL BOY, who has been
sitting at the NARRATOR'S feet listening to the story,
has fallen asleep.)*

FOLEY: TINY BELLS

RADIO ANNOUNCER: *(Enters, holding up applause sign, and the audience continues to applaud.)*

Wasn't that an inspirational story, preparing all of our hearts for the celebration of Christmas! Truly wonderful. Thank you, cast and crew. Let's all give a warm round of applause to our guest star today, Biiiiill Landry [your actor's name]!

(Holds up applause sign.)

We would also like to thank Wampler's Farm Sausage Company again for its generous contribution.

SINGERS: *(Enter and invite the audience to sing, too.)*
WAMPLER'S, WAMPLER'S, IT'S GOOD SAUSAGE. MADE ON THE FARM IN TENNESSEE. DON'T SAY SAUSAGE, JUST SAY WAMPLER'S FOR THE BEST IN QUALITY.

RADIO ANNOUNCER: *(Holds up applause sign.)*

Wampler's Farm Sausage—a family tradition since 1937. Remember to include Wampler's Sausage in your meal planning this holiday season! All of us at the Lyric Theatre Sound Stage would like to thank Wampler's Farm Sausage Company for sponsoring this segment of The Christmas Tree Angel Radio Drama, and now…

(Holds up applause sign.)

…as we sign off the air, we ask that our live sound stage audience join us in singing the Christmas carol, "Joy to the World." You will find the words to the song in your program.

(EVERYONE on stage encourages the audience to join in the singing.)

EVERYONE: JOY TO THE WORLD, THE LORD IS COME! LET EARTH RECEIVE HER KING. LET EVERY HEART PREPARE HIM ROOM, AND HEAVEN AND NATURE SING, AND HEAVEN AND NATURE SING, AND HEAVEN, AND HEAVEN, AND NATURE SING.

JOY TO THE WORLD, THE SAVIOR REIGNS! LET MEN THEIR SONGS EMPLOY. WHILE FIELDS AND FLOODS, ROCKS, HILLS AND PLAINS, REPEAT THE SOUNDING JOY, REPEAT THE SOUNDING JOY, REPEAT, REPEAT, THE SOUNDING JOY.

HE RULES THE WORLD WITH TRUTH AND GRACE, AND MAKES THE NATIONS PROVE. THE GLORIES OF HIS RIGHTEOUSNESS, AND WONDERS OF HIS LOVE, AND WONDERS OF HIS LOVE, AND WONDERS, WONDERS, OF HIS LOVE.

(RADIO ANNOUNCER holds up applause sign and lights fade out, including the "on air" light.)

End of Play

What they're saying about
30 SHORT PLAYS
FOR PASSIONATE ACTORS...

"Lisa Soland has here assembled a wonderful collection of short plays. If you're a passionate actor, a teacher or a director looking for a play to do, you won't find a better place to start looking than this book."
— *Lawrence Harbison, Senior Editor, Smith and Kraus & Applause Theatre & Cinema Books*

"Lisa Soland's amazing collection of 30 excellent, sooo entertaining short plays is a must for any would-be playwright, actor or acting group!"
— *Tom Sawyer, novelist, playwright, screenwriter*

"This collection of plays is as varied and eclectic as the human mind itself. They are funny, dramatic, poignant, shocking, outrageous, satirical, imaginative... It's a must-have for writers of short plays and a great resource for theatres that produce them."
— *Peter Colley, playwright, screenwriter, librettist*

What they're saying about
SERGEANT YORK: THE PLAY

"It's simply a wonderful play."
– Deborah York, Executive Director of the Sergeant York Patriotic Foundation and great-granddaughter of Alvin York

"Sergeant York: The Play is… a powerful statement on the nature of war and the power of faith."
– Peter Colley, playwright/screenwriter/librettist

"I thoroughly recommend *Sergeant York: The Play* for any organization seeking an inspirational, wholesome tale of a true American hero."
– Burt Rosen, President and CEO of Knox Area Rescue Ministries Knoxville

"Soland has devoted her significant abilities to share the story of Alvin York's deep personal faith and commitment to Jesus Christ."
– Sam Polson, Lead Pastor of West Park Baptist Church

What they're saying about
DR. BISCOTTI & THE HUMAN CONDITION

"Lisa Soland's *Dr. Biscotti and the Human Condition* is a tour de force and a masterpiece. Its theme centers on nothing less than life's reasons and randomness. Characters represent the fourth dimension—time rather than space. By the end of the play, we learn how life can differ for an array of people, all linked by the interlocutor—their therapist, Dr. Biscotti. This play is original, entertaining, at times shocking, and brilliantly crafted. Dramatically, it has surprises and a wonderful build to a shocking conclusion. I could not get it, or the deep philosophical and sociological issues, out of my head for weeks after seeing it. I am a long-time fan of Ms. Soland, but this is perhaps her deepest play. I would love to see it get all the attention it deserves."
– Andrew Bonime, Feature Film Producer

"Absolutely riveting dialogue and characters. *Dr. Biscotti* is an excellent work. I was absolutely captured by the characters and their stories."
– Steven L. Sears, TV Producer/Writer

What they're saying about...

INSPIRED!
A Drama With Music

"Inspired! **is a testament to Soland's mastery of taking difficult historical material, drilling it down to the raw emotional truth, and humanizing it in play form. It is bold storytelling of extreme challenges of faith, renewed strength, and the creation of six now-familiar hymns. Soland's** *Inspired!* **makes it impossible to casually sing them ever again."**

– Melanie Ewbank, Producer, Actress, and Playwright

"Lisa Soland has devoted her significant abilities to writing and sharing her new play *Inspired*! **The inspirational stories of these seven hymn writers include John Newton, Louise Stead, and Martin Luther. All had deep personal faith and commitment to Jesus Christ."**

– Sam Polson, Lead Pastor of West Park Baptist Church

"I loved *Inspired!* **Playwright Lisa Soland has done an amazing job once again. She's captured the heart and soul of what these hymn writers were all about. Every scene is captivating and deeply moving.
I couldn't put it down."**

– Deborah York, Executive Director of the Sergeant York Patriotic Foundation and great-granddaughter of Alvin York